Say When

the room is still
pulsing in time to the beat of my heart
the thoughts that race in my mind
demanding answers I can't give
and all that's left is the waiting
for answers that may never come
my heart pounding, waiting
straining for the moment
you say when
all that I need to hear
the words you utter
may break or make me
as my heart races with the waiting
neither soaring nor breaking
the tension taking its toll
till the moment
you say when
knowing my heart is in your hand
waiting till you say when

With or without

The gentle caress of your lips
The tenderness of your kiss
Says everything that your words could never
The rapid thud of your heart next to mine
Keeping time with mine
As I explore you
You explore me
Sharing that last piece of myself
Giving you freely what no other
Will ever have of me in this life
The embrace of your arms
As you move in time with me
Gliding beneath the sheets
Glistening from the intensity of my love
The ecstasy in your eyes
Drives me wild
Makes me work a little bit harder

To hold on just a little bit tighter
Kiss you just right
Make you never want to stop
Make your body sing
The only thing is
This is all in my head
Cause you never knew
Just what I would do
If I were with you
I can't help but wonder
What you might say
What you might do
If you could see my thoughts
Understood how much I want to be with you
The saddest part is you may never know
Because all I want
Is for you to be happy
With or without me

Not Alone

as time moves on
few things change
though we try to struggle against it
fight to keep what we had
the youth of yesterday fleeting
the loss of our beauty
the ugliness of our vanity coming to the surface
from the depths to which
we all pretend to have banished it
but as time goes on
we find that there is more
more than money, than looks, than brains
those around us that become part of us
come to define us
help to remind and revive us
that we are not alone
as I sit in the dark
mind racing and unable to stop
sleep not coming tonight

I hope that you realize the truth
of my words whispered in the wee hours of morn
when the world is still asleep

Void

sleepless nights spent
trying to decipher the yearning
to find the reason
to the feeling
that somehow something is missing
that all is not right
slowly the feeling fades
begins to be acceptable reality
till that glance from across a crowded room
an unexpected smile
a gentle embrace
that reminds us that we are more
that what we do here counts
for more than just us
and the void that
stood before disappears
to be replaced by love

Linger

Days come and go
But my thoughts linger
On the perfect curves of you
The smile that stops my heart
The caress of your lips
Bringing me to my knees
Leaving me senseless
And all I want to be
Is the same to you
So can we linger in this moment?
Just a little longer
Hold on just a little tighter
Kiss like we mean it

Hug like we need the lack of distance
No matter the circumstance
And know that thoughts of us
Linger with you too

Chosen
Thoughts flood my mind
overrun my heart
There is no refuge from the onslaught
of the emotions that fight to be heard
The words that besiege expression
The one thing I can't fight
The time between you and me
The silence that fills the space between us
The doubt that maybe I'm not enough
And so the war continues
Do I say what I really mean?
or something in between?
Do I trust that you feel the way I do?
That I could be enough for you
My heart has already chosen you
But my mind can't believe you'd want me too
So everyday is a struggle
But I've made my choice
And it's you

Dream

the feel of your lips on mine
plagues my mind
leads it question
all I things I've kept inside
not quit hiding
but not truly revealing
the deeper essence of feeling
boiling just beneath the surface
though it may seems shallow
at first glance
the love I profess
being the truest kind
the love of you
not just the magnificent trappings
but the soul of you
as my soul longs to linger with yours
my heart aches to go on
without you here
as you are inevitably
the deepest part of me

the best part of me
and in my mind I see
that shallow though it may seem
this physical outpouring
of my soul is my greatest
protest of my affection
and till I see you again
I shall dream
Of your kiss

Exception

Every day feels the same
since you been away
and I hate how it changes
whenever you're here
cause I cant deny how I feel
you're my exception
to every rule
I just want to be
your exception too
Every time you smile at me
I almost forget to breathe
doesn't matter what I do
and I just keep on waiting
for the day that you see
you're my exception
to every rule
I just want to be
your exception too
its the way you laugh
its the way you smile
its everything about you
it drives me wild
you're my exception
to every rule
I just want to be
your exception too

Warfare

With every breath I search for the words
The acts to define the emotions that rage

Within me the sight of you invokes in me
My joy at the sight of your beautiful smile
The way my heart breaks to know your pain
My heart breaking to hold you till you finally see
There is nothing I wouldn't do to love you
Be loved by you
So I sit and try to rhyme my tired words
The words that will never express
The way I feel about you
The way the sun doesn't quite shine
When you're gone
My soul feels incomplete when you not near
And your so damn amazing I'm scared
Scared that someday you may just see
Just how fucked up I can be
And want to leave and yet
I know my heart has never loved another
The way I love you
And in my soul I know the truth
And in that instant my heart is at ease
Knowing all it needs to know
Bearing that love is patient
Kind, is never envious or selfish
Never seeks to please itself
Is neither proud nor rude
Love keeps no record of wrongs
Never delights in evil but rejoices only in truth
Love always trusts hopes, always trusts, always perseveres
And never fails
Bearing that all in mind
I must profess
With all my heart and soul that
I love you
And I know that love is not an emotive
Or an empty word but a verb a choice
One I have made
And will fight to show you
Both now and forever

Facade

the fear is building in me
tangible, breaking in
finding the doubts that plague me
tearing the walls of confidence
I seek to hide behind
the shreds of truth I built upon
can't be just more lies
still the doubts nag
and break upon the edge of my mind
relentless as the tide
undeniable
you are not the one I need
but I cling to the facade I wish to see
the facade of you and me

Catalyst

in the silence that surrounds me
I search for the catalyst of the changes
 at the heart of me
for the moment I decided
who it was I was going to be
the moment I decided to never give in
to fight and win
to never let go of the best pieces of me
those pieces that make me unique
that tie me to my sanity
and lead me to uphold my integrity
and as my mind searches it
continues to come back to you
my catalyst

Masterpiece

maybe this is love but it seems so hard
like the pieces just don’t want to fit
no matter how hard I try to find her
the one I need just keeps running away
and so I keep trying to build this masterpiece
but it just wont come together without her
all the signs pointing to the truth
I always knew, just tried to hide
that things are better
whenever we're together
and it's pretty clear when she's on my mind
from the moment I wake
till the moment I sleep
that I got it bad

Gone

take a look around, and memorize this moment
the look in my eyes in the instant that I know
remember how it hurts and then watch me go
because I can promise it would be the end
no more time spent wondering how you feel
if this feeling inside of me is worth the risk
that you might break me and leave me
unwanted, for something I'm not
take a look around and notice
the lack of tears in my eyes
I refuse to let you tear me apart
make me feel used and dejected
unwanted and defective
memorize this moment and know
that I love you more than anyone could
but I wont be the second string
forever waiting for a chance at the real thing
take a look and realize that this time I'm really gone

Invisible

what would it take to get you to see
that I'm more than just some guy
when I say I love you
I'm not lying
I would drag the mountains down to the seas
bring the moon if that's what you need
to believe, I would be anything you need me to be
what is it I never said, never did
why am I so damn invisible to you

Truth

in the end is it better to know a lie or the truth
the lie that is so much more appealing
the truth so much more dangerous and unfeeling
a lie can bind where the truth can break
and a lie can cover many mistakes
but the truth is always right there
waiting to be seen, callous to the facades of our dreams
the truth will always be there
the question becomes
does anyone care to see
what hides behind the lies
the reasons we use to justify
in the end the truth is all that stands
for those with eyes to see

One

the tears that are spilling from your eyes
are screaming apologies
and the first reaction of my heart
is to remind you I love you
no matter what you do
whatever we have to go through
I'm rite here and Imp never leaving you
as my hands dry your eyes
my heart strains to show you
what I see, the most beautiful girl
the most amazing soul
and I find that all I want is to hold you
till your tears are gone
to help you feel whole
the way you make me feel new
with nothing but a smile
and make my soul soar with your embrace
just let me be
that one for you

Restless Slumber

Silent hours fill tireless thoughts
Lifeless eyes long forgotten, awake I ask
When will I tread another path
Admire true beauty, find a better friend
Somehow the voice screaming yes is weak
the still small voice is all I seek
the silence abounds with screaming in my
mind all there is, all there was, all there will be
You fill my thoughts from my waking moments
to the instant I slumber soundlessly
But for now I'm just consenting to this sense
this sense of restless slumber with you in
my mind again

Tick tock

The clock ticks
My mind ticks along in time
All the while with you in mind
The smile that lights your face
The way your eyes say what you mean
All this comes to me with all of the history
of Love and war
but in your eyes I find
Myself whole
Complete

Bad day

perfume lingers on my pillow
your warmth still radiates to my core
your caress touching the very soul of me
till I remember you're gone
I'm here but you
Your gone and it looks like just another bad day
Again

Moving Mountains

my soul is crying out
that I can't keep this up
that I can't keep trying so hard
but I cant give up on this
I cant turn away from the stirring
you cause in my soul
even if that means I have to move mountains
cross oceans, bring you the moon
I can't quit now, so here I am
trying to move mountains
bring you the stars and help you see
just what I'd do for you
the best part of me

Complete

the minutes tick by into hours
days and years
the constant that remains is you
the beauty and grace of your smile
the light in your eyes
the caress of your lips
the embrace of your arms
when you know its time for me to go
the way you never seem to want to let go
and I cant help but smile
at the thought of you
and know that when I see you
everything will be alright
the longer I'm gone the more I realize I need you
more than the air I breathe
you are the one I need
to be complete

The eyes of an angel

I have seen the eyes of an angel
An angel who saw everything in me
smiled and said love is unchanging
An angel took my hand and showed me
that love is not just something we feel
it's something we commit to do
to find our needs in second place
to another, that is love
I have seen an Angel as she walked away
I felt the pain that broke me
but still I knew my need was to love
I have seen the eyes of an angel
the eyes of Hope
and it is therein that I love

fear

Silent fear surrounds
enters without limits or bounds
buried beneath the surface
hidden behind the smiles
the witty eyes, is the subtle truth
the fear that bides
am I enough?
If I speak the words I feel
the ones I fear
will they run, laugh
or will they turn to embrace
to show that I am
enough

Questions

the thoughts resound in my mind
the overwhelming why
what makes me the one to trust
why I can't seem to stop trying
fighting to make sense of everything
between us, everything you share
and how I feel about you
never seems to change
but I can tell you aren't as sure
of who I am

Reminiscent

words surround me as i stand here
watching you just smile at me
you're so damn beautiful
I can' help but to smile
and my mind starts racing
reminiscence brought on
by the fact that you're near me
the way you looked at me
the way you kissed me
like you may never see me again

Purgatory

The thoughts thunder inside me
Besieging my mouth to move
to spill forth the words inside
that go left unsaid
left forgotten swept under the rug
the point of the words long lost
hangs in the space between
waiting to be set free
from the purgatory of thought
to become words
actions that say more
that move and shape the world around
and the struggle to
let loose the words that bring peace
continues to be
while it never seems hard to lend voice
to the pessimist in me

Still

How can I find my way to you
thru the maze that you have cast around you
to protect that piece of you
that has been broken and bruised
that has been misled and you used
how do I show you that I want nothing but to love you?
Hold you and show you what I see
every time I look at you
the one that makes my heart ache
with a whim
the casual phrase
the words that remain unsaid
but here I am all over again
picking up pieces left behind
trying to show you how much more you deserve
and yet you seem to always see rite past me
as if I'm not really there
when the walls are crashing
but I cant turn away from you
not while my heart aches to hold you

Lost

Lost in thoughts
That never end
Thoughts of expectations
Calculations and computations
Filling the space of thoughts
That lend to humanity
Thoughts that assuage my soul
How to define my morality
The worth of a man
The emptiness that beats in my breast
Where my heart should be
Why more and more
Things that mattered once
Just don't anymore
And how less and less
You cross my mind
Thinking to myself that I'm scared
That I'm losing myself
But not feeling anything
More afraid that I'm numb
And I don't know why
But I'm still searching for that
Somewhere I belong

Know

Every night as I lay awake
My mind gravitates
To you and reminds me
How I just want to be in your arms
Your head on my shoulder
Far away from everything
Around me in this living dream
So far away from the one thing
I know I need
That I don't want to live without
Refuse to live without
Can't be me without
And I hope that far away as you are
You're lying there
Thinking about how you can't imagine
Life without me, us, whatever that is
Whatever you call it
I just know that I need you

Hope

what I'd give for this moment to last
to see the light dawn in your eyes
in the instant that you finally start to realize
that I mean what I say, that I'm not going away
that I love you yesterday, today, tomorrow

Waiting

the air is still, but electric
as I memorize this moment
you and me , together, happy
now I wait for you
the warmth in your eyes, staggering
the longing in your embrace
its power overwhelms me
now I wait for you
you spill your secrets, and cry
I dry your tears and remind you
that I wait for you

Broken

The silence is staggering
the weight of all the words never said
the phrases that could have so easily mended
It's funny that I was there when you needed
tried to piece together all your reasons
your rhymes, tried to understand the whys
why you could never seem to see that when you disappear, you take a piece of me with you
I wonder if you even care that I would move mountains for you,
but of course I can see that in the end I'm just the safe one,
The one you run too but not the one you run home too,
I see that I'm good enough to share the skeletons with but not enough to share a life with,
I'm through with the games and the lies the bullshit and the disguise,
I wonder if you'll even know I'm gone until you break down again

Mystery

Every sense tells me to leave
but I can't seem to move past you
The words that were said
the lies that were so craftily thread
as my mind begins to still
I wonder did I ever mean anything to you
still I cant see how you could be so cold
break me down to nothing, standing there so bold
but in the end I will solve this mystery of you and me
In the end if you want someone but not me
I can guarantee that is how it will be
And you will never find someone like me again
That guy that you haven't seen for years
call me up spilling tears over some other guy
and still somehow makes her smile
never to be the one but always the one that wants the chance
to love a girl like no one before
The mystery that I just can't solve
how can I be enough to trust
the one who knows the skeletons in the closet
but not the one you trust to love you best
the one i trust enough to see the real me
the you that only you see
I can't trust you more than that
why is it that you can't trust me back
it's just another mystery
same as you and me

Not quite whole

the seconds drag on like lifetimes
in the absence of you
the world is not quite right
when you aren't by my side
I'm not quite whole
the smile I flash isn't real
the look in my eyes makes it clear
I'm just not the same without you here
and in the absence of you
I write these stunning melodies
and string along beautiful words
to chase away these thoughts
of me minus you
to keep you in my heart
despite the miles that keep us apart

Never Before

the silence stretches on as we lay here
the words to express what I feel won't come
It has been so long since my heart has burnt so bright
this love consumes it, and it breaks every time
I have to leave, My only thought becomes when I will see you again
and I try to find a way to show you how I feel
so that when I say I love you
you already know that I do
and as the rain falls around us
and the world conspires against us
I smile despite it all, cause as long as you are here
things just seem a whole lot more clear
and I know why I'm here
I here to love you
like no one ever has before

intoxicated

I can feel the smile pulling at the side of my mouth
when you look at me, I cant help it
your eyes hold mine
and my voice catches in my throat
and I force a breath as I struggle to find the words
to express this need
to close the distance between you and me
and pull you close to me
sweep you off your feet
and leave this world behind
and as I reach out to take your hand
the world just seems right
in this moment, in this light
and I grin as you take my hand
and lean you head against my chest
listening to my heart as it thunders
in my chest intoxicated by the proximity of you
straining to tell you this love is true
That I love you

moments

as you sit there studying
I cant help but stare
and the thoughts that flood my head
how when I'm around you everything changes
in these moments when I'm with you
these moments that change the world
the way you smile at me
your beautiful laugh
the scent of your skin
it's in these moments that I truly live
these moments I share with you
where all I see is you
while we sway gently to the music
as I sing sweet melodies
to bring out that breathtaking smile
that sets the world on fire
the look in your eyes that draws me into
a whole new reality
inhabited by just you and me
and I never want to leave
these moments with you

dreams unfold

my dreams unfold around you
sitting there so sweetly
you smiling asking me what I'm staring at
to which I can only reply
the most beautiful woman in the world
and as you blush, I pull you close
wrap you up in my arms
and sing sweet lullabies
as we sway gently
I kiss you so sweetly, you can't let go
because in that instant when my lips caress yours
you know where my heart lies
you feel the strength of the love that ties
every time you look in my eyes

Cracked and Bleeding

the silence is shattered in the midst of the screaming
the words flying back and forth stopped having meaning
and all that's left is the feeling, the anger, the fear
everything that comes before the tears
and the moment when you break
fall apart, realize there's more to this heart
than jut some jaded shattered parts
left behind from all the mistakes of the past
left behind by all those, "this time it will last's"
leaving a heart that's never really whole
a heart that always feels a bit cold
cracked and bleeding, and yet still beating
broken down but not defeated
and this is what I hold in my hand
a heart that has been through the ringer
broke down making it hard to linger
but I place it you hands
and pray you don't break me apart again

Single one

Thoughts running through me
millions at a time, against the backdrop of my mind
all returning to single one
how I hate it when I have to leave you
all I want to do is hold you close
sway nice and slow to the music in my mind
as I sing sweet love songs to you
keep you close to me
write poems that can only be epics
to keep me in your thoughts
the way you dominate mine
turning the corners of my mouth to a smile
just by walking into a room
without words making me want you
to notice me, see you the way I do
and know that my love is true
cause all I need is to be with you

Choke

The words won't come to me
they're stuck in my throat
choked off by the beating heart
that once resided in my chest
and I try not to stare
but your smile is so breathtaking
I can't tear my gaze away
and in this moment, I just want to sing
everything, anything till you notice me
see my heart straining to beat it way out of chest
to present itself to you
to express to you that you are more beautiful
than the sunrise and the sunset
and more graceful than an angel
and in this moment
I would give up forever to touch you
cause I know that you feel me somehow
and for now all I want is for you to know
who I am, so I take a deep breathe
whisper to myself maganda ka
and pray I don't choke
in this moment
this moment when you are so beautiful I could die
I just want to know you
want you to know who I am

Die

the air is cold as the door closes
leaving me shivering and alone
as I search my soul for a reason
to explain away the pain that is tearing thru me
refuses to abate within me
leaving me shaking with silent tears
streaming down my face
trying to stop from breaking to pieces
trying to be strong, but the emotions pour on
like a typhoon drowning me
till I am forced to say fuck it
take a deep breathe and just go with it
and as the waves subside I find that place inside
and slowly pull together those pieces that are left of me
and do all I can to glue it back together
still knowing I'll never be the same again
never truly mend, till I learn to let you go
and that is a challenge, that I not sure I can defeat
but for you, I will do anything
even if it means I have to die inside

piece of your soul

Breathe in all the change
look around and see how nothing is the same
notice how nothing lasts forever
but nothing much was meant to
but when all the lights fade
and the moments have passed away
there are always the memories
that drive the present, shape the future
define the reality we confine ourselves too
and in the end the memories fade too
leaving just the dim reminder of a feeling
tied to a moment, a picture, a sound
that comes on whenever they come around
and It hurts like hell
but you forget how you survived before
forcing all the voices telling you to stay away
into the dark away from the light of day
knowing there right but not caring anyway
falling again the same as every other day
till you realize it will never go away
because it's become part of the whole
a piece of your soul, a piece that makes you whole

Regret

And this is the moment that I know the moment I fall apart,
broken shattered on my own left to contemplate
the mistakes I've made to understand the way I let you walk away
the greatest thing that ever happened to me
was the day you showed true love to me and like a fool,
I let you slip away gave up the fight,
too scared to ask do you love like you did
would you come back to me and In this moment
I understand the fault is my own
I gave in when I should have never let go
you were the world to me
but in the end it's his world you'll complete
and through the tears that stain my cheeks I will smile, knowing that you have found that piece knowing that you are happy, complete

just one kiss

I take your hand as we sink gently
into the sweet embrace of the leather couch beneath us
we are just one kiss away from bliss
my lips gently caress your hand, with all the love I have
and you envelope me in an embrace so sweet
I forget to breathe, and all there is in this moment
is you right here next to me your lips intertwined with mine
saying all that words never could, In that moment
I am complete, with the proof that I am a part of you
and you need me too, just a bit more than you might want to admit
a little scared by the overwhelming sense of it
in this moment to know that there is only one word
That I can think to utter between breaths
I love you, uttered with more passion than
you would have imagined possible
until I uttered them to you
and as I pull you into the sweetest kiss
I feel you melt into my arms
and I just want to live in this moment
till I die, with you here by my side

Need

the sun sets on another day
and still I'm so far away
with a million thoughts running through
all of them revolve around you
the way your eyes light up when you smile
the way you look at me
the way you speak
everything about you is perfect to me
the longer I'm away the more I know
that there's not much I need
but you everyday
to hold you in my arms
to say I love you more than the air I breathe
to pull you close and sing sweetly in your ear
to kiss you so tenderly that you go weak in the knees
and protect you from everything you fear
to be everything you need
the way you are everything for me

All I want

the thoughts run rampant in my mind
filling the space, filling the time
and I'm just sitting here wondering
how after all this time you break me apart
with all the walls that stood between
you just shatter every line of defense
between you and me
and all that with just a smile
a sparkle in your eye
a sweet hello, a quick goodbye
and I spend the next small eternity
thinking of everything I had to say
but just couldn't, How I just want to be with you
wherever you go, whatever you do
whatever it is that would make you see
all I want is you to want me

couch

it's like magic the way look at me
see thru what the rest of the world sees
and then find a way to bring it out of me
and with a single look I'm frozen
too beautiful for words
when we talk I can't get you out of my mind
for days, and when I do I close my eyes
and there we are on the couch
that marvelous creation
the birthplace of my fondest memory
and when I open my eyes
all I want to do is run to you
hold you in my arms
and remind you that my love is strong enough

You

as the rain trickles down my face
I stand watching the window pane
hoping it's the day, hoping it's that moment
the one I can't help but dream about
wondering what's taking so long
singing softly out loud
I'd give up forever to touch you
cause I know you feel me somehow
and all I need is one moment
to prove that this is real
the whole nine yards
every second of everyday
I will be right here, waiting
till you answer the door
let me in, and let the love begin
with a simple kiss
that is so intense you can't resist
the kind that makes me forget everything
but you

scared

what I am to you is not what you need
when sleep beckons me I close my eyes
but still all I see is me and you
not quite the perfect fit, but I could never quit
never let go of someone so beautiful
so comfortable with all of me
hating that you cant seem to
see that we could be so much more
not perfect but what the hell is
All I know is I want you too damn much
to give in, so what's it going to be
a string of guys that aren't even close to Mr. Right
or can you give this guy the time of day
would that be alright, or are you just scared to try?

Grenades

as the sun sails out of the sky, words dance and weave in my mind
the sky lights up with diamonds, breathtaking but still missing
the piece that makes my soul soar, with eyes of hazel
and the smile of an angel, that haunts my dreams
makes the deepest part of me yearn to be more
to turn the world upside down, burn it to the ground
go to hell and back, and the yearning is always there
held in check by the smallest thread of self control
but on nights like these when I'm oceans away from you
I let slip that thread that holds me together
break down and let loose the parts of me that are so weak
my need to see you smile at me, the way you do
the way you make me stop and say I love you
with the words you drop like grenades
tearing apart the defenses I set to keep this desire back
knowing that it's not quite reciprocated, still I'm standing here hoping
someday maybe, but the longer I stand here the more I think I'm just crazy
but my feet can't carry me away from you
and my soul won't relinquish these thoughts of you

The end

as I close my eyes I face the wave of memories shaping me
pulling and dragging me in their wake
causing my knees to shake and my heart to quake
bring the soul in me awake and my heart to bare
leaving behind every shred of fear, knowing as i stand
in the wake of my memory I do not stand alone
I cherish the hand I hold, my anchor in the storm
making me bold enough to take on the world
and there is no way I would let go
come hell or the end of the world
the hand I hold is the only thing I need to remind me
who I am, and in the end she knows who I am
and with that I can face the end of anything

I do

sunset fades as I turn and walk away
my mind reeling from the thoughts that play
as the sun sinks behind the mountains in front of me
I close my eyes and begin to see the mountains between me and you
days come and go, as I try to tear down every one
bring them to the sea and cross the bridge I made to you
ready to be smooth and suave, ready to prove that I'm new and improved
never stopped loving you, the cathartic charge that drove me to become more
than I was before, enough to make you want more
hold me closer than every before and hear my heart
as it tries to beat its way out of my chest
as my soul stands there screaming here I am
please take me as I am, let me be whole again
when the fuck does the waiting and growing end
when I'm enough to hold you close and love you
more than anybody has ever, to prove how much
I do

Proof

In the cold loneliness that exists in the hours before the sun awakes
my heart, mind, soul grasp for a shred of proof that I am not alone
as I reach for the phone, the debate rages in me
the nagging doubts that you won't give a shit
maybe I'm just to fucked up and scary enough to make you quit
in this moment I just need you to know who I am
to know that someone sees me for what I am
no more, no less than a man
with his heart in his hand, waiting for a woman
to take my hand, and except me as I am
flaws and all, as the phone rings
I bottle the fear that runs rampant in me
and when you answer with a soft "hey" that way you do
my heart skips a beat and I begin to believe
maybe that proof is you for me

Swallowed by the sea

in the stillness of my restless slumber
I feel the hole you left in me
as my heart races to deafen me
telling me one thing in an endless string
that you were meant to be with me
not swallowed by the sea that stands between
that distance that dwarfs all things
the distance that only time brings
and I wake for the millionth time
I force a deep breath and push you from my mind
knowing that the moment I close my eyes
it will be the same typhoon of memories
that rages inside me, bringing my heart to brink
left desolate and wasted by each fresh wave that breaks

Beating

in the stifling silence of this oppressive solidarity
I fend off mountains of memories
that hurt like a bullet to the brain
as the memories pour like rain
washing over me in an endless medley
bringing tears to my eyes
and as the saline rolls down my cheeks
I can't help but smile
at all the times that I surprised you
when you shot my heart with some new truth
and I'd smile and look you in the eye
and return with a smooth reply I love you
how at the end of the day you knew who to come to
that I will always be there for you
with my heart battered and bruised

bleeding and a bit used
but still beating for you

Destiny

the sky is filled with diamonds
blazing in the night before me
as the stars fill my gaze my mind drifts
thru a cornucopia of memories
each a piece of a masterpiece
of tragedy and love and war
that blend together in harmony
thread thru past and present
beyond to future destiny
and I laugh at how little things change
but in the end its all really just the same
tired old song and dance
stuck on replay struggling to break the cycle
to master it's destiny

The Island

as my eyes flutter open
I take stock of the world around me
finding that I am alone
on the path untrode
with only one way to go
forging my way thru
working my way to something new
feeling the change brewing
with each new struggle urging me on
to redefine who I've come to know
what I've come to be
facing on my own
the Island within me

Abba

this distance is crushing me
leaving me breathless
struggling to keep my head up
to pull together all the reasons I'm here
struggling to hold in the tears
as the waves come crashing again
endless as the sea, wearing on every ounce of me
dragging away all the pieces I strive to be
and suddenly its crystal clear, that I cant do this anymore
and my soul is already crying Abba
as my knees sink to the cold floor
and in the moment I surrender to you
I feel the strength of divinity's embrace
as your hand brushes the tears from my face

fairytales

from day one we are told who to be
what to wear and who to see
bombarded by relentless sentiments
to dictate how to love
and find the one
the chase and the catch
but the forgotten piece
when the one is caught
what then I pray of thee
these fairytales of love and woe
that we have woven to keep
us safe and warm
thru the willful bending of time
need some careful mending
and better happy endings
because we all deserve more than
the next best thing

Home

thought twist and wind their way through me
haunting me, pulling me apart from within
as I fight to hold on to every piece of sanity
I close my eyes and breathe deep
bringing my heart to bare, forcing my way to the crux
this nagging fear and doubt that refuses to cease
hostilities against my heart
tearing at me, leaving me scrambling to find shelter
and the miles between me and peace seem inconceivable
my soul cries to be home
to rest in the haven that gives me the strength to be
my soul longs to be whole again
to know it's worth is seen
to be home again

More

the seasons warp and cycle through
as I continue to struggle to find the catharsis
that will break me of my need to be
anything other than just me
to bring to me the strength to be
nothing less than what I strive to see
when you look at me, the way you do
To be the one to never let you down
the one to get rid of the frown
never let you hit the ground
because thru all these seasons
you have been my reason to be
more than just what the rest of the world sees

Refrain

The days drag on slowly
as my soul screams it mantra
How long, in endless succession
with no cessation in sight
so tired of playing along
sick of this tried old song
am I not smart enough, not sweet enough
not strong enough, is it me?
and in the silence of my deafening thoughts
I marshal my resolve
to never give in
to never let the world get the better of me
to keep tearing down all the obstacles in my way
and never letting complacency sway my heart
till the refrain comes again, and I fight
to keep the saline from rolling down my cheek

Angels

weary thoughts birth tired words
and my mind races, pulsing in time
to the deluge of questions that drive me
searching for the answers that will
solve the mystery of this life
the sense that all is not right
that we are not quite whole
the answers in the eyes of angels
hidden from view
echo silently through my soul
the question that will never cease
the one that will see my soul
and hold my heart
know my faults and still stand fast
steady with love that's true

Entity

Day in day out
I strive to find the way
to be more than this
shattered and alone
broken and torn
struggling to divine
how to redefine everything I am
and pull my heart back from the flames
tearing apart every thread of love in me
leaving behind only apathy
I search desperately
for what would make me
a singularly whole entity
no longer broken and empty

Just beneath the skin
to the one who changed everything

boiling just beneath the skin
the terror of letting someone in
past the secrets and lies
close enough to see the scars
left behind, showcasing my brokenness
shaping the image everyone sees
the wholesome version
edited and incomplete
the reality a little more bent
warped and full of grit
and as I struggle to gain composure
I left the fear wash over me
Hoping who I am
is enough
as I stand here my imperfections
flood over me
and all I can do is smile
and hope all the while
that I am enough
knowing my choice is right
I hold out my heart

Diversity

as I look around I try to decipher
the rhyme uncover the reason
that no one seems to see the beauty
that is so plain to see
waiting to be seen
screaming and pleading
staring at the world
through every season
of the human condition
the best parts of all of us
that somehow end up overlooked
undervalued, leaving our faith shook
isn't it about time that we stopped
fighting to hide the beauty
of our diversity?

Words

as my heart pounds in my ears
I ransack my vernacular
struggling to find the perfect phrase
to capture the feelings that rage
through me when I see you
pulling at my heartstrings
like a marionette
I dance around the point
that my heart demands I make
while the whole of me trembles
in anticipation of the moment you know
how I see you and what it does to me
every time you have to go away
leaving me wanting more

Uncertainty

silently I drift among an ocean of mysteries
clambering to find my way
knowing the beauty that lies within the uncertainty
and the time to dig deep has come
force my fear to the side
and lay my heart bare
as I sit, wishing, waiting
patiently praying
for the chance to be that one
to be more
than just some friend
more than something to which you attend
as my heart sits bare
and I sit wishing, waiting
to be the one you never want to go
the one you strive to know
as well as your own voice
and here I sit wishing, waiting

The whole of me

As I stand before this precipice
of my indecision
to let you into the whole of me
the parts that no one else sees
the parts that haunt my dreams
and as I struggle to speak
I take my heart
and place it in your hands
knowing words don't mean much
hoping that my heart is enough
and as I teeter on the edge
I begin to realize the only thing left
is to take the plunge
give in and let love in

shades of grey (breathless)

shades of gray cover my eyes
leaving me blind
as I struggle to decipher
what you are to me
more than a friend maybe
someone I love possibly
these shades of gray
fall over me
leaving me to fend off the shadows
in front of me
that push and pull at me
telling me who I was
who I should be
as I struggle to be free
of these shades of gray
all I know is that you move me
force me to improve piece by piece
what you see
and through these shades I gray
I see myself falling into you
as I yearn to know all I can
about this mystery that is new
who are you, what is it about you
that leaves me breathless wanting more than I ever have before

Soldier

the world keeps tearing apart everything
no matter how hard I try to finish this
there's always that one step left
one more piece to the puzzle
so I keep on moving
pushing thru the next trial
to find they never really stop
so as I hold on for dear life
I lean on the best parts of me
the ones that make every day
worth what the world makes me pay
so I cant give up now
too many reasons to never give in
and just as many to make me sing
laugh and cry, and never once forget why
in the end it's what makes me
this soldier you see

evade

thoughts echo in my head endless
across my mind vast as the sea
the waves ebb and flow
and the tides of thought churn
I watch as my perceptions warp
and change, light and catch flame
and as they go up in smoke
I try to find the things that matter
amongst the incessant sputtering thoughts
bouncing around my mind
keeping me from finding peace
as I try to put together all the pieces
that I call my life
I find the answers I seek evade me still

Beautiful

wandering thoughts wind in and out of my mind
leading me to the question of what you see
when you look at me, stacked up with all my faults
am I enough to hold your heart
as I wonder I cant help but smile
the smile lighting up your face
as your eyes find mine
and I feel my heart jump a little bit
at the beauty of you
body and soul all the way thru
and as I stand and stare
I wonder what you see in me
hoping you see the love in my eyes
and the warmth of my smile
and know what i see in you
the most beautiful woman of all

Absence of you

in the absence of you
the world seems so much duller
less vibrant and wonderful
so much colder than before
and I can't seem to remember why
I ever let you say goodbye
but it was the worst mistake
I will ever make
in the absence of you
I have lost all that made me whole
all that kept me from drowning
in the sea of my inadequacies
because in you rest all those things
in you rests my hopes and my dreams

safe bet
as life fades away day by day
certain truths blossom like a bouquet
bringing with it wisdom that was hidden
veiled from my eyes secret and unbidden
the strength that I once thought I had
seems suddenly useless in the light
of this sudden omnipotence
knowing that I have been so blind
neglecting the most vital part intertwined in the heart of me
the reflection of the love that is given free
each and every day by those that are everything to me
reminding me of what I seek
who I am completely myself unique
with the burning desire to show the world
a love that will bring it to it knees
begging for more, longing to appease the brokenness
that is apparent in the vistas
that we desperately seek to hide behind with closed fists
because love is never the safe bet, the easy way out
but it's worth every single bout

Because of you

in the space between thought and dream
I close my eyes and smile
played out like a movie scene across the world of my dream I see you,
in the moment we first knew
that despite everything our love was true
the days I sang to you when the sun was asleep
and all the things I wrote to move and woo
when life seemed simpler and a hug was deep
and meant more than words could explain and as
I drift away till morning I smile to myself because of you

with me

the world closes in on me
drawing in closer every day
tightening its grasp on my life
trying to crush every facet of my dreams
till all that's left is a bruised and battered shell
of all I aspire to be, but it can never take from me
the love you've given freely for all to see
your love that courses through these veins
and makes me feel strong enough to entertain
the schemes the world lays against me
as long as you are here with me
I can take on the world
one day at a time

Enough

the deluge of thoughts is constant
every time I close my eyes
the downpour of thoughts
that flow in me despite all I do
leave me weak and crying
sick of lying to myself
that I'll be alright
I fall asleep and dream of what I could be
what I would be, should be
but I know that I wont be
till I decipher the manic cry of my heart
that screams to be heard
above all the ruckus of my thoughts
incessant and relentless
in the corner of my mind
I begin to see that I may never be
what I dream
but I have only ever calmed the noise in me
with the presence of an angel in guise
of the most amazing friend
that personifies Hope
that I can be enough

the greatest thing

as the days drift into years
and what was disappears
to become something shiny and new
my heart yearns for you
and even if we are worlds apart
I cant still the beating of my heart
sometimes I wish I knew what to do
all this time I've been searching for a way to you
to find the part of me that was everything
the reason my soul would sing
and as time is the king of most everything
the exception is the crazy sensation causing this beating
in my chest that I cant put to rest
as time holds sway over most all things
but not of the heart or the songs it sings
love my dear is the greatest thing

debate

as the sun rises
my soul stirs with endless queries
and dredges up tired old theories
used to define and explain
the human condition
lending to the building of my own predispositions
of measuring the value of everything within
and so continues the tired game
that never really ends
the tally that never stands
in my favor, by my own standards
that at times feel archaic and oppressive
but that have served me well
yet my soul burns with an obsessive need
to exceed my own limitations
to set forth grander expectations
the dire need to be more than I seem to see
the resounding debate that resides in the core of me
am I enough?

Rain

as the rains begins to crash down again
my mind brings to me
the memories that hide within
calls at three in the morning
ending with me singing
you goodnight
laying on your floor
with your mom scolding us in the door
when a hug meant more than anything
the kind that could make any day amazing
just by having you in it
how you looked at me when I kissed your hand
and as the rain ebbs and dies
I dry the tears that have escaped my eyes
and try to pretend that it won't happen next time
I hear the rain crashing down like a chime

numb

the air is just a little bit colder
the room just a little darker
my mind numb , left dumb
staring at the hole in me
coming to grips with reality
the lose of you and me
despite being better together
the storms we couldn't weather
and the lack of you
is killing me slowly
from the inside out
till all I am is numb
unfeeling and dumb

shadows

when the shadows settle
on my weary skin
I ask myself where to begin
my mind a myriad of thoughts
comprised of you
The warmth of your smile that soothes my soul
the love in your eyes never grows old
the embrace of your arms so desperate
like my embrace can alleviate the pain in you
every night the shadows settle in
my heart begins a coup
alas as the sun springs anew
my mind takes over and relinquishes you

anchor

the world assuages me endlessly as the sea
with trials and tribulations that shake and shape me
yet through all these I keep sight of my anchor
that weathers all the storms of my soul
that undeniable fact that cannot be shaken
that faith I have in you
the faith you have in me
the world may bring the end
but it will never break my faith in you
my anchor at sea that keeps me
from being lost at sea

go ahead

never thought I'd be the one
to say it's over and done
but even I can’t deny
love isn't in your eyes
you can go ahead and cry
But I’m saying goodbye
you can go ahead and cry
but this is the last time
so say goodbye
cause I won't be back this time
you never cared for me
but maybe now you'll see
what you really need
Is what I tried to give
you can go ahead and cry
but I’m saying goodbye
you can go ahead and cry
but this is the last time
so say goodbye
cause I wont be back this time
Never thought I'd see
your tears spilling over me
but even you can't deny
that it's too late to try

resolution

in the oppressive silence
left in your wake lies a resolution
to find haven against the world
in the embrace of your arms
the safety I find in your eyes
as they search mine
finding everything that I try to be
the assurance of your smile
telling me I'm enough
leading me to believe in this resolution
that where I belong is in your arms

truth

in the end is it better to know a lie or the truth
the lie that is so much more appealing
the truth so much more dangerous and unfeeling
a lie can bind where the truth can break
and a lie can cover many mistakes
but the truth is always right there
waiting to be seen, callous to the facades of our dreams
the truth will always be there
the question becomes
does anyone care to see
what hides behind the lies
the reasons we use to justify
in the end the truth is all that stands
for those with eyes to see

catalyst

in the silence that surrounds me
I search for the catalyst of the changes
at the heart of me
for the moment I decided
who it was I was going to be
the moment I decided to never give in
to fight and win
to never let go of the best pieces of me
those pieces that make me unique
that tie me to my sanity
and lead me to uphold my integrity
and as my mind searches it
continues to come back to you
my catalyst

Perfect

from the sidelines I watch
as the people around me scramble
struggling to be something
anything more than just enough
fighting to find the magic concoction
of this and that
to be perfect to someone, anyone
but as I stand here watching the people scuffle by
my mind kicks around the million dollar question
who's definition of perfect are they prescribing to
and who decided that was the way to go
why can't anyone be happy with what is
instead we struggle to make everything this utopia
that was handed down to us by everyone that came before
never wondering why this is the desire in the depth of our hearts
who decided we should want this, choose to depart
from that which is already beautiful
evident to those with eyes to see the beauty of ugly
and the nature of everything that is imperfect
and the beauty of it all

Faking

sitting here in this place alone

my soul wrestles with what is missing

why I continue to feel less than whole

battered, broken and alone

wondering when does this song end

the tune is tired and the words grate into my soul

leaving it barren and cold

waiting for the moment when I am safe

in the arms of the one that moves me

shakes me to the core

breaks me of my apathy

forces me to see, what I try to hide

is there for everyone to see

in the way I smile

and hide my fears and shed my tears

in the way I stumble thru

and In that instant I know

what my mouth has yet to utter

out of fear, out of doubt

that I'm not the one you want

but the time for faking is over

this is real , and I need you

Listen

listen thru the roar around you

the blaring flamboyant distractions

look closer past action and reaction

work out the reasons behind the rhymes

stop rehearsing the same bored lines

feel the urge within to be known for more

than the next guy, to be remembered

as the guy who turned the tide

brought down the sky

crossed oceans, traveled far and wide

to be the one to stand beside you

took you hand and showed you a love that was true

listen closer, to the love in front of you

Peeling

the paint is peeling from the walls

exposing the heart beneath

broken, bleeding, not whole but healing

not sure if I can pull down

the blocks I put up to keep everyone out

when she tore out my heart

left me cold, full of doubt

but what if its time

to let you in

to show you the man I am

broken, but not beaten

fighting to keep it together

working to be better

as the paint peels from the walls

Messy

the road stretches before me
between who I am
and who I want to be
growing longer with every step
paved with the best intent
but always somehow leading to an inevitable descent
into the deepest darkest parts of me
dragging to light the worst constituents
of my battered soul
knowing the path requires that it be laid bare
before it can be repaired
dragging my marred heart through the mud
reminding me that life is messy
less perfect than glossy daydreams
but just as glorious in its imperfection

Sanctuary

the words roll off my tongue with ease

at odds with my racing heart pounding in my throat

as I commit to the memorization you

and I begin to enjoy the bliss

of the sanctuary in every moment spent with you

feeling the fear melt away

as I share the darkest facets of my soul

watching your beautiful eyes

for the instant they reveal any trace of trepidation

at the flaws in the core of me

terrified of the instant it sinks in that I'm so broken

holding this heart in my hand

ready to give you all that I am

if you can take me as I stand

waiting for you to take my hand

Charade

the lights hum as I sit still and listen

to the steady stream of thoughts within

sifting thru memories of conversations past

searching for that perfect phrase

the words that will leave you breathless

wondering what comes next

when I finally come clean

and let the charades we play fall away

like a forgotten game children play

leaving me without a stitch of pretense to hide behind

and so I carefully plot every line

knowing that I get only one shot, one try

so I wait for the words to fall in to place

that will tear the charade away

to show what is hidden just beyond my stoic face

my heart beat running a race

to be the first to be with you

Ruin

If you looked in my eyes would you see
past the facade of plastered smiles
the words crafted to beguile
pull you in and push you away
afraid that you might see
the paint peeling and the chipped ceilings
the broken pieces of my heart scattered about
this place of ruin, buried deep
with all the secrets I work so hard to keep
locked away from the piercing recognition in your eyes
when you see how fragile this heart of mine truly is
would you believe my tried and tired rhymes
that you hold this heart of mine
as I hold my breath and wait for the inevitable part
when you decide just what to do with my heart

Shattered

as the words fade around you

I see the comprehension hit

the tears just starting to spill

saline glistening down your cheek

blurring the sight of me as I make my escape

from the mess we made of life

shattering the moment you were hoping for

after you closed the door

forever never seemed so long

as the sun sets on another night

I hold back the emotions raging inside

roiling beneath the surface, tarrying

for the moment that I break

and finally concede how deep you cut me

when you watched me go

Rebirth

heed the pouring pounding, tumult raging inside
as the rain cascades around you
bringing with it stinging beads of clarity
dragging your contemplation
to the deluge of sordid memories
that lay in the squalor of the darkest moiety
deep within, always kept under lock and key
far from prying eyes that vainly seek
for that missing piece, the chip they can't help but see
in the way you carry yourself in everything
not quite sure of what people will think
hiding in plain sight, buried deep
covered over all the scars that keep
you from being more, keep you yearning
for absolution just beyond reach
of the brokenness entombed so deep
that you cant recall how it even got there anymore
feel the deluge of the rain around you
breathe in deep let it go, let the torrent wash it away
let the rain soak thru you
and feel the rebirth within
as the rain ebbs away

Shoebox

The tattered box that sits on the shelf in your closet Covered by the space between the years since last it's been seen The sacred shell for all the memories that burn to keep Yet refuse to leave your mind when you lay in bed praying for sleep Knowing as you turn over for the hundredth time that it won't Grudgingly relenting to pull down the tattered old box Fully aware of the power it holds, hoping this time the memories don't feel cold Steel yourself and peel back the lid that holds the memories in Breathe deep let the walls that keep the reminiscence back fall away Breathe in the moments that lay buried in this tiny sacred box The way it felt to see that smile that stopped my heart To see that you comprehend all that I am in those amazing eyes Feel the love wash over me with the way you say my name And the tears start to fall as I imagine the way you held me Like you were afraid that if you ever let go I'd be gone And my heart can't help but skip a beat when I recall The caress of your lips so soft and sweet That perfect moment where I felt complete And just as the feeling strikes the reality crashes Down around drowning out all my lucid memories And I remember why the tattered old box sits In the back of the closet on the shelf But as I slip it back into place I can't keep the grin off my face

There Is

Look again at the world before you
See past the plain and the evident
See thru the haze that settles around you
As you make all the right moves
And play the game called life
So eloquently fooling everyone you see
See past the plastered smiles
To the tracks of tears
The half buried fears hidden for years
In the faces around you
Just waiting to be seen
Open your eyes to the beauty around you
In the imperfection and brokenness
Of those that surround you
Every scar telling another story
Of diversity lending to the beauty of the scene
Spread out before you
Bent broken hearts that refuse to quite beating
Breathing and tearing apart every wall they meet
Till it's plain as day that with every beat there is love

The Waiting

the waiting never seems to end

the hollowness that gnaws at me

making every morning a battle

to crawl out of bed, put on a smile

pretend that the emptiness is defunct

when the truth is that it's left me numb

leaving just me and the waiting

to feel anything but numb

kicking and screaming to be rid of this sickening apathy

that has settled itself over me

waiting to see past the bent and broken in the mirror

to remember how it felt to be seen

and be held in the fragile arms of my dreams

before the first few rays of sun break thru my sleepy haze

and the battle begins again

the waiting is on again

Scars

the darkness settles in as the sun drifts again beyond the horizon

falling away with all the grace of the stars, leaving behind only the days scars

fresh and deep they cut anew sculpting you over again

leaving traces of the moments that you cherish

that you lock away with the knowledge they make you who you are

while each new scar adds a new layer, to the shelter you've built around it

forcing out everyone along the way

scared shitless that someone may just see past to the real you

raw and unabashed, naked for all to see

the core of your entirety, calmly facing the eyes around you as they seek

for the answers that you can never give

to the questions that they could never ask but always want to

and the awkwardness burns in this moment

will I stand here unflinching trying not to look away

as you search thru everything that is me

waiting to hear you say those simple perfect words
that trifecta of acceptance

Bricks

the memories shift in the twilight of the dreams that surround me

dragging me under in the current of things I thought I'd forgotten how to feel

the emotions raging in me till they are all I can hear pushing and pulling at me

and all of sudden you are all I can see, the piercing gaze of your eyes

that see rite through to the core of me, the way your hand fits perfectly in mine

and the peace that settles over me when your arms gently envelope me in that hug

that never ends, one part comfy two parts scared that maybe it will be the last

and these moments keep assuaging me out of the blue, breaking me apart every time

forcing me to brick the holes you left in me back up again till the next onset

of memory sets me adrift in this ocean of recollections that are slowly killing me

that I cant let go anymore than I can ask you to go

Happy Ever After

The lights fall slow and steady

Same as every other day before

But there is change in the air

Quiet but palpable, working it's way thru

The fabric that has become happy ever after

Leaving behind smiles that are slightly less

Embraces that are less than whole

Missing that yearning that was in your soul

The beginning of the ending, creeping up

Breaking apart the laws that make the world work In the back of your

mind gnawing at the something wrong

And how to get back to happy ever after

Immortal

The thoughts drift away as the sweet release of slumber pulls me under bringing with it a beautiful barrage of memories that have been tucked away buried deep but daring after the light of day, dancing dubiously before my eyes Leaving no escape from the bliss they create in the ache that has settled in my heart making my heart beat a little faster, my breathe catching at the allure of your eyes full of comprehension of the man staring straight back at you the love that courses between palpable and leaving us forgetting to breath all that matters is you next to me your hand in mine my heart in yours both now and forever more And the moment lasts a lifetime and is gone in an instant as all dreams are fleeting but immortal, as the feelings they dredge up in me, leaving me closer to whole than before

Shell

There is a war raging inside of me no one else seems to notice, the scars that mark every outcome chipping away at the heart of everything that is whole in me, leaving behind small truths and white lies that compose the face in the mirror The face the rest of the world sees But there is no fooling you, no fooling me as you stand by the choices that have brought us to this place I wonder if mine have all been mistakes if my resolve to be unique have made me incomplete left wanting and obsolete to those around me leaving behind a distinctly lonely shell of a man with a painted smile that doesn't quite reach the eyes the trace of tears just beneath the surface the brokenness evident in the soft bitter strokes of the words I paint every picture with and yet there burns in me a fire a small fearful desire to find everything that I've been missing to return a better man, completely whole again

Spinning

Listen closely to the unspoken goodbyes As the thoughts slowly come to grips with reality Of the choices made and what they mean The haze that was just a bit of distance before Just opened up to become a chasm before us And the yearning in the core of me doesn't die Just slowly subsides lingering without need Paying no attention to the caution I excersize Dragging my soul thru the broken torn pictures and Shattered frames of dreams that we're always there Buried deep in me, and the control I have begins to seem unreal To see that in the middle of the dreams I built up in my mind Crashing around me lit up and burnt down by the choices you made You really are happy and somehow I am too And reconciling that just won't happen loving you Was always so complicated and just when I thought my heart had given up Left you to the happy ever after you chose But things never seem to be so cut and clean Not for you and me, and as I try to stop the world spinning I realize that it will always be that way between you and me

Hiding

Breathe in, taste the change all around
swelling up from the inside
where all the inhibitions have locked away
all the sharper edges of your singularity
falling away leaving glimpses of what we could be
shockingly beautiful in its stark contrast to the abridged version
that the world sees whenever they glance at you
Stoic and in control, pleasant and whole
hiding the scars that defy the image portrayed
the emptiness running to the core
leaving nagging doubt in its wake
making every day a struggle to appear as happy as the day before
running on the fumes of the hope
that you cling to like its your final lifeline
praying that no one breaks thru the facade
to see how broken you really are inside
afraid to have to appease prying eyes
Knowing the moment is inevitable
still its scary as hell, to let anyone else in
to leave them a heart to break in two
when they decide they don’t really love you after all

Hollow

The space between the words spoken and those buried deep but burning to be free The dissonance of the space between carves out a hole in me leaving behind a heart that is hollow bleeding, broken, but beating warring with every breathe to leave you behind my mind suffocated by the thought of it to lose this precious piece of me the game changing earth shattering elements of me that only you bring out of me stoking the fire of my desire to be more than just another forgotten face from some distant time and place pulling apart the walls in the darkest expanses of my soul to what makes me whole as you stand there with you arms around me I fight to keep this wave back but it's like trying to hold back the sea and it's crushing me the weight of the words unsaid all that's left is to succumb to the tumult inside to give in and let the words crash around me Hoping you know just what I mean Sure that you have seen how hollow this silence has made me

Let me in

As the lights go out around me my thoughts drift through the deepest darkest corners of my mind forming sweet harmonies from the memories dancing before me coloring my dreams with the richest melodies The beauty in the smile that lights my world on fire The depth of your gorgeous eyes that search mine holding me locked in that instant of space and time drawing me into a place shared by just you and me a secret world where all the facades and charades are left behind because they mean nothing here where truth is everything, so hold on tight cause the truth is so much stranger than fiction so much more potent and scary as hell too but your love is worth every risk so here I stand praying you will start again with the heart I'm holding in my hand bruised but not quite broken, still mending from love lost but ready for a new start waiting for you to let me in

Buried

the silence that has settled over us has become so natural
both of us so careful not to broach the walls
that hold back the deepest feelings that run between us
and the silence isn't that bad at all
what is really killing me is the numbness
that has crept into the way we speak
idle chatter when before we spoke of everything that mattered
delved in the crux of who it was we wanted to be
and the memories that have always been so beautiful
now burn a little bit in the back of my mind
but I will never let them go
because the burning cuts thru the numbness the silence leaves
and reminds me of what I need
to be whole all over again
to leave behind what was and may have been
the best thing to ever happen to anyone
and so the writing and the drinking comes
to begin the journey to get away

from the broken pieces to rebuild
find the truth buried in the midst of the burning
that surrounds these memories that make me unique
that prove that I will always be there for you
whatever life drags us through and the choices
that inevitable pull and break us apart
you will always carry a piece of my heart
deep in the corner of you heart
and I can tell its true when I look in your eyes
feel in the way you hold me in your arms
when its been too long, and you know there's a piece
of you walking around with me too buried in my heart

Happy now

so many memories haunting me
pulling, pushing, tearing me
everyday wont let me be
and this question keeps driving me
when the lights go out
and you're there in his arms
when the lights go out
are you happy now?
so many words left unsaid
hanging in the silence
so thick its deafening
and the question keeps driving me
when the lights go out
and you're there in his arms
when the lights go out
are you happy now?
can you really smile so sweetly
when all the lies subside
and the charades die ?

so many what ifs spinning
round in my head
waiting for that one word
and the questions keeps driving me
when the lights go out
and you're there in his arms
when the lights go out
are you happy now?

All That Glitters

slip out of the world around you
and into the world you dream about
when everything was easy as breathing
words didn't go unspoken, they were just understood
and time was so inconsequential, as long as there was you
when sleep wouldn't come the phone invariably rung
and in the space between that separated us I spilled
all that my heart held into words gilded in song
to convey that everything would be ok
I will never leave, never run away, never stop loving you
even when we are both old and gray
and as we slip out of the dream that enfolded us
there is still one thing you can always trust
that when you see that all that glitters isn't gold
I will be right here waiting for you

Secrets like shots

it was always so easy to see
what was hidden to everybody around us
the beauty of your soul
staring straight at me in you hazel eyes
captivating me till I realize I forgot to breathe
pouring secrets like shots, straight to my soul
pulling me deeper into you
with no end in sight, no need to fight
as I let slip the darkest lick of my soul
as our secrets intertwine, combine
with the exchanges of trust
a language of our own is discovered
where a look says all that words never do
and a hug says so much more
as our worlds collided to create more
than our dreams could ever hold
the haven that lies in you eyes, your smile
the gentle, yet overwhelming embrace of your arms
that assert this is where I belong

Fading

As I sit watching all the people pass by
Thoughts converge in my mind flowing through me
Washing gently from you to me and everything between
Breathing in all the memories from now to then
Wondering where I lost myself along the way
Because the man in mirror is a stranger
The eyes a bit harsher than I remember
Seeing less wonder than before
And the soul therein beaten to the bone
Weary of the journey, but still nowhere near home
And everyday I could swear I feel pieces of me drifting
To the great beyond, leaving me facing a stranger
Losing myself slowly to the necessity around me
Pushing harder, going longer, doing everything right
Constantly pushing aside the parts the world doesn't need
Shaping who they need me to be and
I begin to realize I hate the man
That is fading away before me so fragile and weak
No will to stand and fight anymore
And in the end some of the best of me just fades away
As I become what everyone else needs
The fear dissipates in the shelter of your eyes
Your arms that show me I belong
As I fight away the fear that I'm losing every part of me
Your smile reminds me that as long as you're here
The best of me can't really fade away

The boy

Night falls again just the same
Feeling the cold rush in
Waiting for the feeling to fade
Wishing I could wake up
To more than the space you left behind
Leaving me wondering
What do I have to do
How the hell do I prove
That I'm not myself without you
That my heart won't beat
Without your arms to keep me sane
And I would tear the mountains down
Drag them to the sea, rip the stars from the sky
And bring you the sweetest melodies
To soothe you to sleep, if that's what you need
Night falls again and the dream is the same
I'm standing here heart in my hand
Asking the girl if I can be the boy
From this day till the end

Scream for more

Somewhere in between the shadows, the road I thought I was on
Fell away, and I feel the dirt crunch beneath every uncharted step
Still not sure where I'm running to just feeling the urge to move
To get away from where I'm standing, feeling raw and exposed
Waiting for that fatal bit of truth to shatter the shell I've built
Pushing out all the doubt and the fear, to create something more
Than just the next man, striving to build a heart that can take a beating
Pass thru the ringer and keep standing believing, in the destiny before it
The purpose that has been set in the core, pulsing with every beat
To fight and win every second of every day, to leave a scar on the world
That will always be remembered, so I pass the days striving to be unique
But whole, carving a path never strode before; daring to believe there is more
And everyday proving just little more that I am strong enough to bring the world
To it knees without a single shot, it's all in the strength of my heart
As the days fade away I feel an ache to return to the melodies that set me free
Taught me who I was meant to be delving into what I needed creating a haven
A place where every move is ok, and all that matters is the heart that beats in you
And the ache inside to share something beautiful that will change the world
One word at a time, with a melody laced with intensely lush melodies that sing
Straight to the soul, cutting to the core

Brokenness in me

the tears spill freely, pooling around me
like so many shards of weakness pouring out of me
leaving behind a shell, a husk that is so fragile
a gentle breeze would collapse it
and the tears cascade again, as the night fades on
in the absence of the love drug in my veins
and boiling just beneath the skin
the anger roils, pushing out the fear
and the self pity that feels so ugly
as i try to reconcile the panoramic view
of who I've grown to be
and the disappointment crashes down in waves
the eddies pulling at the shreds of belief left in me
till I can barely stand, forced to sink
and the breathe wont come, as the doubts flood in
and the affirmations fade away, clouded by the critique
that has been building deep down within
hidden underneath the heart beating within
breaking slowly but never ceasing to believe
because there is you, and you still believe
in the brokenness that exists in me

Mirror mirror

lend an ear to the half truths passed around
the white lies used in vain to disguise
what lies before our eyes, the edges are more jagged
behind the veil of secrecy strewn throughout our monologues
and the question burns, what the hell are we so afraid of
we all have scars buried deep inside
what is so scary about the truth
the moment we come clean, step out into the light
finally ready to be seen, imperfect but beautiful
wholly unique, yet with all we are we fight
to be something less than honest
afraid to accept our deepest flaws
trying so desperately, to scream
mirror mirror on the wall
I'm the fairest of them all
to blinded by our lies to see
that we are all broken and jaded on the inside
few of us strong enough to see it and move on

www.ingramcontent.com/pod-product-compliance
Ingram Content Group UK Ltd.
Pitfield, Milton Keynes, MK11 3LW, UK
UKHW051136260726
13967UKWH00010B/3090